Settling and UNSETTLING the West

J.B. Caverty

Consultants

Vanessa Ann Gunther, Ph.D.
Department of History
Chapman University

Nicholas Baker, Ed.D.
Supervisor of Curriculum and Instruction
Colonial School District, DE

Katie Blomquist, Ed.S.
Fairfax County Public Schools

Publishing Credits

Rachelle Cracchiolo, M.S.Ed., *Publisher*
Conni Medina, M.A.Ed., *Managing Editor*
Emily R. Smith, M.A.Ed., *Series Developer*
Diana Kenney, M.A.Ed., NBCT, *Content Director*
Courtney Patterson, *Senior Graphic Designer*
Lynette Ordoñez, *Editor*

Image Credits: Cover and pp. 1, 8 (top), 17 (bottom), 23 (top), 25 (top), 27 (front) North Wind Picture Archives; p. 4 Pictorial Parade/Getty Images; p. 5 (top) Washington University, St. Louis, USA/Bridgeman Images, (left) Courtesy of UC Berkeley, Bancroft Library; pp. 5 (right), 31 Kansas State Historical Society; pp. 6, 9, 24-25 Granger, NYC; pp. 28-29 Sarin Images/Granger, NYC; pp. 6-7 Courtesy of the Montana Historical Society, X1952.01.10; p. 7 Public Domain; p. 8 (bottom) NARA [6883912]; p. 10 Ann Ronan Picture Library Heritage Images/Newscom; p. 11 Clark Kelley Price; p. 13 (top back) MPI/Getty Images, (top front) NARA [299808]; p. 13 (bottom) Whitman Mission National Historic Site, National Park Service; p. 15 (bottom) Peter Newark Pictures/Bridgeman Images, (middle) NARA [299809]; p. 17 (middle) Beinecke Rare Book and Manuscript Library Digital Collections; p. 18 (top) Peter Newark Western Americana/Bridgeman Images, (bottom right) LOC [LC-DIG-cwpbh-01671]; p. 20 (top) National Archives, General Records of the U.S. Government, (middle) Courtesy of the Rare Book Division of the Library of Congress, (bottom) University of Oklahoma Libraries Western History Collections; p. 21 Look and Learn/Bridgeman Images; pp. 23 (left), 26-27 Peter Newark Western Americana/Bridgeman Images; p. 23 (bottom) Bridgeman Images; p. 28 LOC [rbpe.01701000]; p. 29 (left) LOC [rbpe.07204800], (right) LOC [LC-DIG-pga-01416]; p. 32 NARA [6883912]; back cover Courtesy of UC Berkeley, Bancroft Library; all other images from iStock and/or Shutterstock.

Library of Congress Cataloging-in-Publication Data

Names: J.B. Caverty.
Title: Settling and unsettling the West / J.B. Caverty.
Description: Huntington Beach, CA : Teacher Created Materials, [2017] | Includes index. | Audience: Grades 4-6.
Identifiers: LCCN 2016034141 (print) | LCCN 2016048209 (ebook) | ISBN 9781493837977 (pbk.) | ISBN 9781480757622 (eBook)
Subjects: LCSH: Pioneers--West (U.S.)--History--19th century--Juvenile literature. | Frontier and pioneer life--West (U.S.)--Juvenile literature.
| West (U.S.)--History--19th century--Juvenile literature.
Classification: LCC F596 .R526 2017 (print) | LCC F596 (ebook) | DDC 978/.02--dc23
LC record available at https://lccn.loc.gov/2016034141

Teacher Created Materials
5301 Oceanus Drive
Huntington Beach, CA 92649-1030
http://www.tcmpub.com

ISBN 978-1-4938-3797-7

Printed by: 590835
Printed in: China

Table of Contents

Welcome to the 1800s. 4

Why Move West? 6

Heading West 10

Unsettling the West 20

A Growing Nation 26

Advertise It! 28

Glossary 30

Index 31

Your Turn! 32

Welcome to the 1800s

The 1800s were a time of growth for the United States. The long fight for independence from Great Britain had come to an end. Now, people were looking to explore their new country. They were ready for adventure. The West was that adventure.

Life on the **frontier** was exciting. Rumors of gold gave hope to many. The promise of land and good farming drew people, too. The West was full of possibility.

But, the growth of the country also caused problems. As settlers moved westward, they pushed American Indians and Mexicans out of their homes.

The 1800s were a time of westward expansion. These settlers paved the way for the future of the United States.

People travel west in covered wagons.

Famous frontiersman Daniel Boone leads a group of settlers to Kentucky.

These ads encouraged people to settle in the West.

Why Move West?

A writer named John O'Sullivan had a huge impact on how people viewed the frontier. O'Sullivan was a smart man. He graduated college when he was just 18 years old. People always wanted to hear what he had to say. So, he started writing his ideas. In 1845, he published an article for a magazine. In it, he said that all of North America should be part of the United States. He said Americans were destined by God to own the land. This idea became know as **Manifest Destiny**. Many people liked this idea. They used it to justify the growth of the nation.

John O'Sullivan

Not everyone agreed with O'Sullivan. They argued that other people already lived in the West. American Indians had been living there for thousands of years. They did not think people had the right to take land from these **tribes**. Still, the idea of Manifest Destiny spread. And so did the nation's borders.

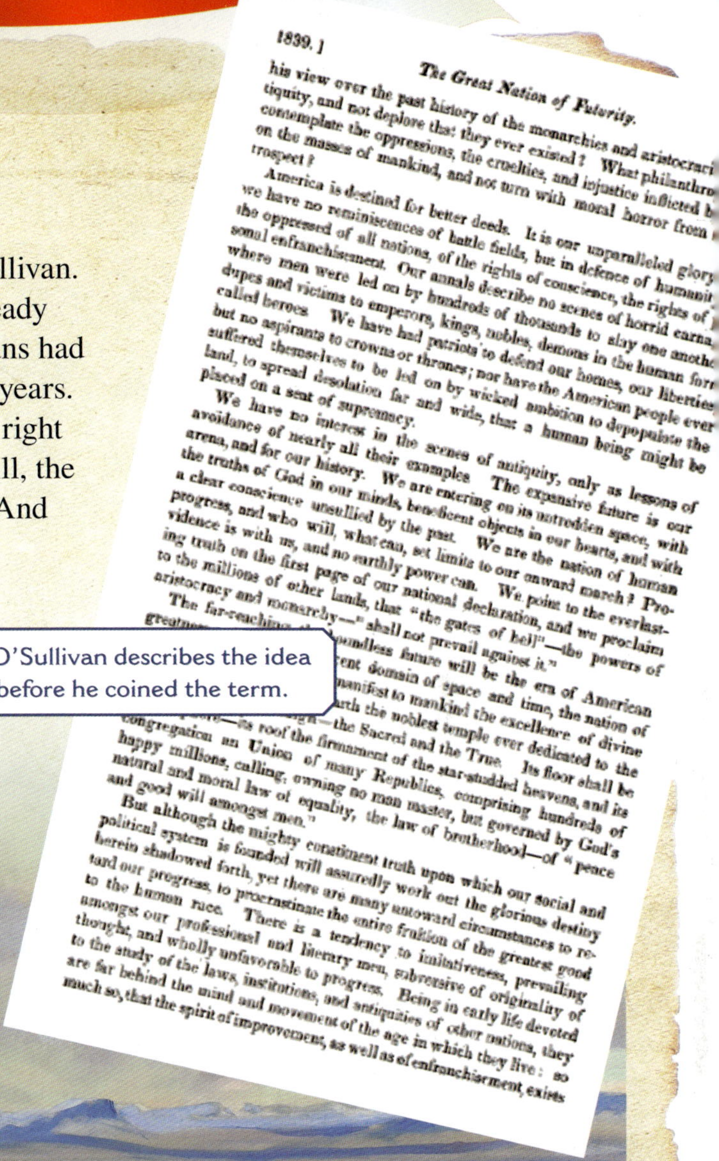

1839.]

The Great Nation of Futurity.

his view over the past history of the monarchies and aristocraci
tiquity, and not deplore that they ever existed? What philanthro
contemplate the oppressions, the cruelties, and injustice inflicted b
on the masses of mankind, and not turn with moral horror from
trospect?

America is destined for better deeds. It is our unparalleled glory
we have no reminiscences of battle fields, but in defence of humanit
the oppressed of all nations, of the rights of conscience, the rights of
sonal enfranchisement. Our annals describe no scenes of horrid carna
where men were led on by hundreds of thousands to slay one anothe
dupes and victims to emperors, kings, nobles, demons in the human forn
called heroes. We have had patriots to defend our homes, our liberties
but no aspirants to crowns or thrones; nor have the American people ever
suffered themselves to be led on by wicked ambition to depopulate the
land, to spread desolation far and wide, that a human being might be
placed on a seat of supremacy.

We have no interest in the scenes of antiquity, only as lessons of
avoidance of nearly all their examples. The expansive future is our
arena, and for our history. We are entering on its untrodden space, with
the truths of God in our minds, beneficent objects in our hearts, and with
a clear conscience unsullied by the past. We are the nation of human
progress, and who will, what can, set limits to our onward march? Pro-
vidence is with us, and no earthly power can. We point to the everlast-
ing truth on the first page of our national declaration, and we proclaim
to the millions of other lands, that "the gates of hell"—the powers of
aristocracy and monarchy—"shall not prevail against it."

The far-reaching ... boundless future will be the era of American
greatness ... ent domain of space and time, the nation of
... manifest to mankind the excellence of divine
... arth the noblest temple ever dedicated to the
... —its roof the firmament of the star-studded heavens, and its
congregation an Union of many Republics, comprising hundreds of
happy millions, calling, owning no man master, but governed by God's
natural and moral law of equality, the law of brotherhood—of "peace
and good will amongst men."

But although the mighty constituent truth upon which our social and
political system is founded will assuredly work out the glorious destiny
herein shadowed forth, yet there are many untoward circumstances to re-
tard our progress, to procrastinate the entire fruition of the greatest good
to the human race. There is a tendency to imitativeness, prevailing
amongst our professional and literary men, subversive of originality of
thought, and wholly unfavorable to progress. Being in early life devoted
to the study of the laws, institutions, and antiquities of other nations, they
are far behind the mind and movement of the age in which they live: so
much so, that the spirit of improvement, as well as of enfranchisement, exists

In this 1839 article, O'Sullivan describes the idea of Manifest Destiny before he coined the term.

a crowded apartment building in New York City in the late 1800s

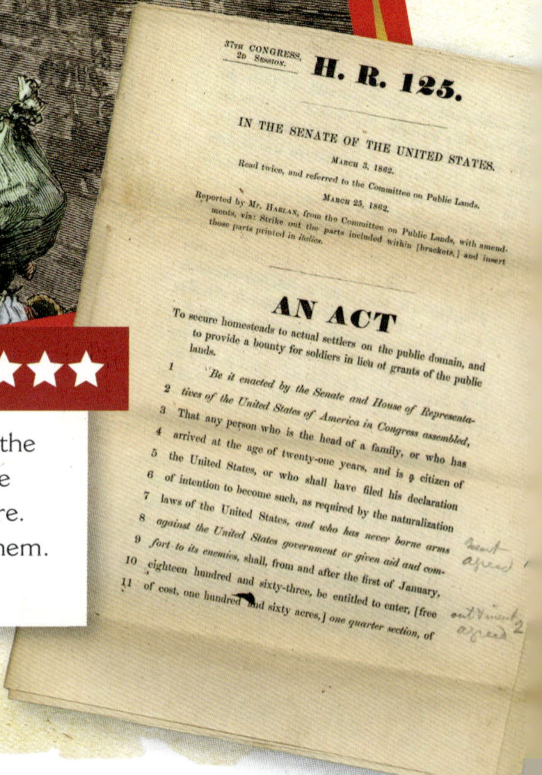

37TH CONGRESS, 2D SESSION. **H. R. 125.**

IN THE SENATE OF THE UNITED STATES.

MARCH 3, 1862.

Read twice, and referred to the Committee on Public Lands.

MARCH 25, 1862.

Reported by Mr. HARLAN, from the Committee on Public Lands, with amendments, viz: Strike out the parts included within [brackets,] and insert those parts printed in *italics*.

AN ACT

To secure homesteads to actual settlers on the public domain, and to provide a bounty for soldiers in lieu of grants of the public lands.

Be it enacted by the Senate and House of Representatives of the United States of America in Congress assembled, That any person who is the head of a family, or who has arrived at the age of twenty-one years, and is a citizen of the United States, or who shall have filed his declaration of intention to become such, as required by the naturalization laws of the United States, *and who has never borne arms against the United States government or given aid and comfort to its enemies,* shall, from and after the first of January, eighteen hundred and sixty-three, be entitled to enter, [free of cost, one hundred and sixty acres,] *one quarter section, of*

LINCOLN'S BARGAIN

In 1862, President Abraham Lincoln signed the **Homestead** Act. It gave settlers land in the West if they farmed it and built a house there. After five years, the land would belong to them. This convinced many people to move west.

a Worchester, Massachusetts, factory in 1855

People headed west for many reasons. Some left their homes because of **push factors**. They hoped the West would help them start a new life. Life in the East was cramped. Big families lived together in small apartments. Factories and tall buildings crowded the streets. These factories were not safe places to work. Men and women worked for 12 hours or more every day and earned very little pay. Some children even worked in factories! They had to help their families earn money.

The Civil War was another push factor. It was fought over slavery and states' rights. Much of the South was destroyed after the war ended in 1865. People looked west for a fresh start.

Others headed west because of **pull factors**. Gold and silver were found in several places in the West. Gold and silver rushes soon followed. People flocked to the West in hopes of striking it rich. Land there was cheap and good for farming. Some people felt **oppressed** where they were. The West offered a chance at freedom. For some, that was worth risking it all.

Heading West

When people traveled west, they usually took their whole family. They went in covered wagons that were pulled by horses, mules, or oxen. Wagons were big, but people still had to leave most of their things behind. Some people even traveled on foot for thousands of miles so they could fit more items into the wagon.

Timing was important when heading west. If travelers left too early, there would be no grass along the trail for their animals to eat. If they left too late, they might get caught in heavy snow. They had to leave at just the right time.

Settlers struggle to get their wagon across a snowy bridge.

ALL ABOUT WAGONS

Wagons were made of wood and had white fabric over the top for protection from the weather. They were 12 feet (3.6 meters) long with wheels that were 6 ft. (1.8 m) tall. People often traveled in long lines called *wagon trains* for safety.

A family buries a loved one along the trail.

Even if settlers found the perfect time to leave, traveling on the trails was still hard. A lot could happen to a person along the way. Some people were run over by wagons. Wild weather could cause wagons to break or get stuck. And sometimes, animals trampled travelers. But, disease was by far the biggest killer. For every mile of the trail, between 10 and 15 people died from disease. Those who died were buried in shallow graves along the trail.

Even with all of these dangers, people still headed west. Their journeys made trails that led from one side of the country to the other.

The Oregon Trail

One of the first routes traveled was the Oregon Trail. Traders and fur trappers blazed the trail in 1811. By the 1830s, it was being used by settlers in covered wagons, too. The trail started in Missouri and ended in Oregon. That's 2,170 miles (3,492 kilometers)! The trip could take up to six months. But, it was better than traveling by sea. That took a year or longer.

Many settlers thought the long trip to Oregon would be worth the journey. Reports of **fertile** land promised good farming. And land was cheap enough for people to start a new life. But, there was a problem. Great Britain had already claimed much of this area. The United States and Great Britain tried to rule the territory together. But as more people came to Oregon, arguments began.

Great Britain and the United States couldn't decide who owned the land. In 1846, the two sides came to an agreement. They split the area in half. The United States took the south and Great Britain took the north. The deal added 286,000 square mi. (741,000 square km) to the United States. The young country was growing quickly.

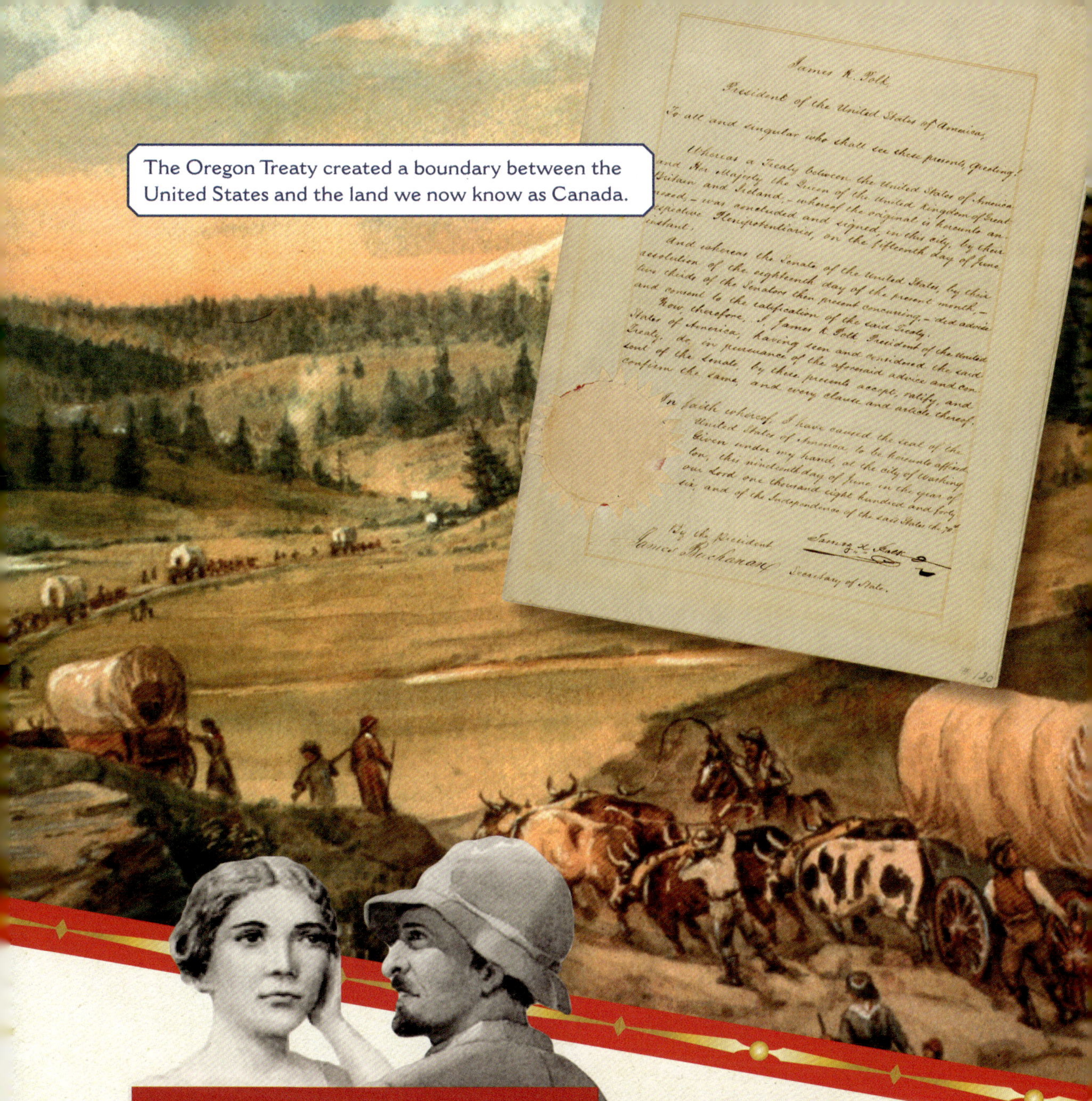

The Oregon Treaty created a boundary between the United States and the land we now know as Canada.

James K. Polk,
President of the United States of America,
To all and singular who shall see these presents, Greeting:

Whereas a Treaty between the United States of America and Her Majesty the Queen of the United Kingdom of Great Britain and Ireland, – whereof the original is hereunto annexed, – was concluded and signed, in this city, by their respective Plenipotentiaries, on the fifteenth day of June instant.

And whereas the Senate of the United States, by their resolution of the eighteenth day of the present month, – two thirds of the Senators then present concurring, – did advise and consent to the ratification of the said Treaty.

Now, therefore, I, James K. Polk, President of the United States of America, having seen and considered the said Treaty, do, in pursuance of the aforesaid advice and consent of the Senate, by these presents accept, ratify, and confirm the same, and every clause and article thereof.

In faith whereof, I have caused the seal of the United States of America, to be hereunto affixed. Given under my hand, at the city of Washington, this nineteenth day of June in the year of our Lord one thousand eight hundred and forty six, and of the Independence of the said States the 70th.

By the President
James Buchanan
Secretary of State.

James K. Polk

MEET THE WHITMANS

Marcus and Narcissa Whitman were two **emigrants**. Narcissa wrote about what she saw along the Oregon Trail. Her letters were published and became very popular. People wanted to read about life on the frontier.

The Santa Fe Trail

Ten years after people began using the Oregon Trail, a trader named William Becknell started another trail. The Santa Fe Trail also began in Missouri. But, it went south and ended in New Mexico. It soon became a **trade route** across the United States. Settlers traded fur from the West for goods from the East. As more people arrived, the trail was used to deliver mail. Settlers sent letters home about finding silver. Soon, more and more people arrived hoping to get rich.

Not everyone was happy with the new settlers. The United States had **annexed** Texas in 1845. But, the western border wasn't clear. Settlers were claiming land that Mexicans said belonged to them. In 1846, the first shots of the Mexican-American War were fired. Both sides fought hard for two years. Then, in 1848, the United States and Mexico signed a **treaty**. The treaty sold over half of Mexico to the United States! The United States paid just $15 million for the land. This new territory drew more people to the Southwest. The Santa Fe Trail was the best way to get there.

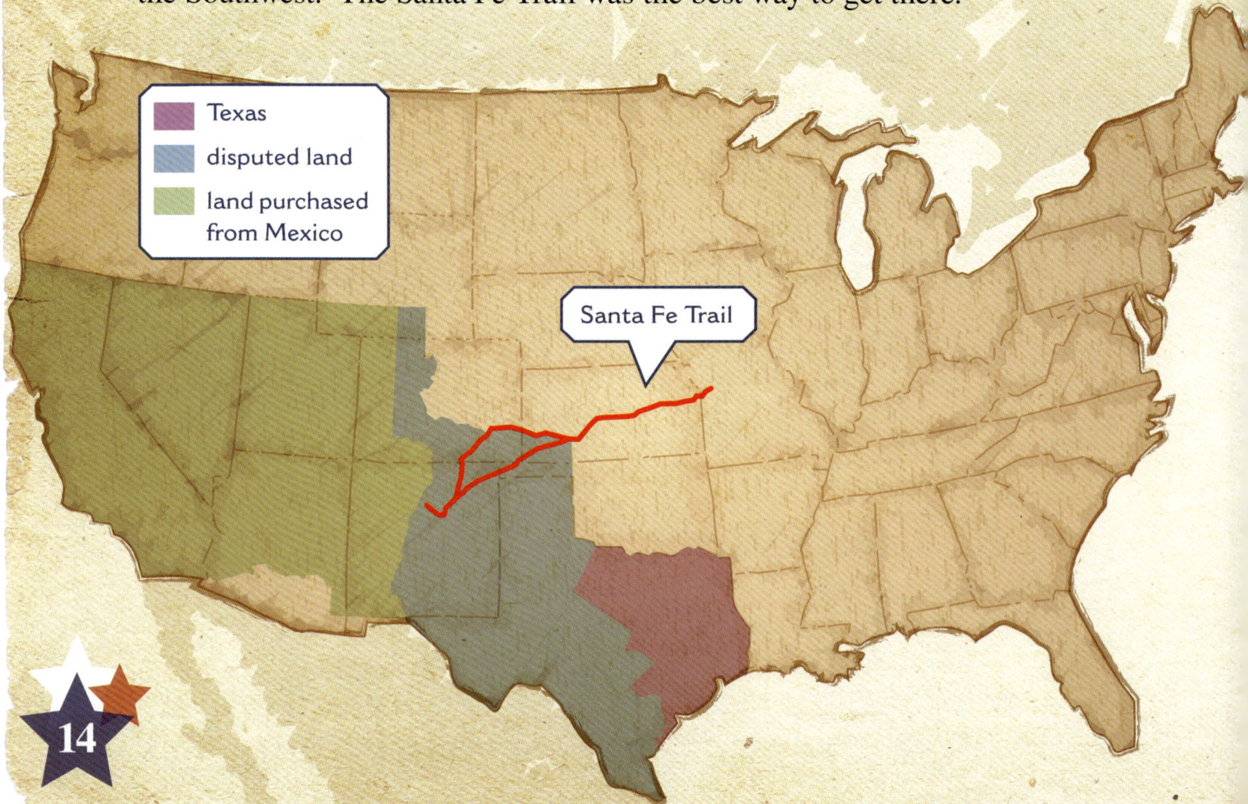

Mexican and American forces battle in 1847.

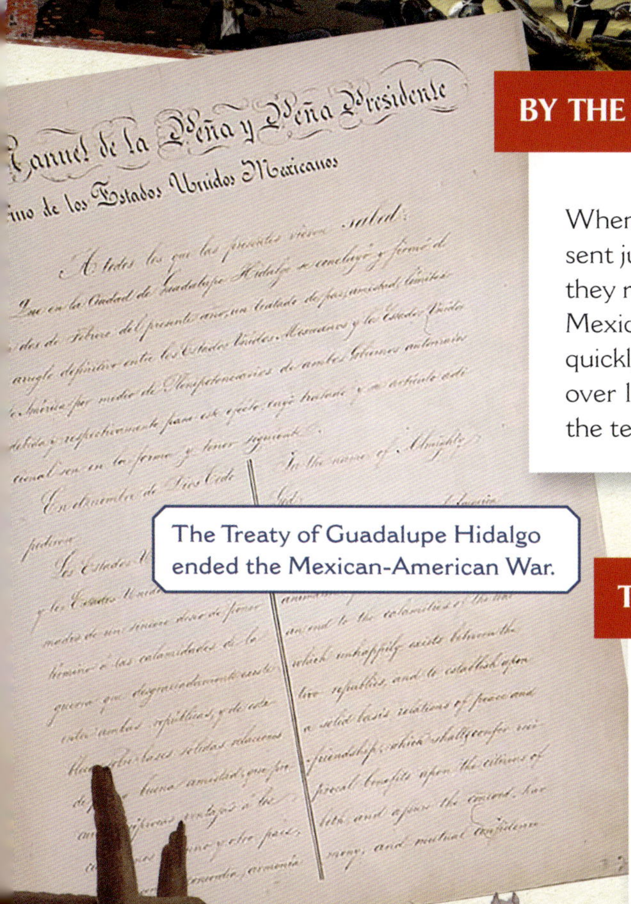

The Treaty of Guadalupe Hidalgo ended the Mexican-American War.

BY THE NUMBERS

When the war began, the United States sent just 5,000 soldiers to the area. Once they realized there were over 80,000 Mexicans living there, the United States quickly sent more soldiers. By 1848, over 100,000 Americans had been sent to the territory.

TEJANOS

Mexican farmers were called *tejanos*. After the Mexican-American War, they found themselves on land that belonged to the United States. Their land continued to shrink as settlers moved in.

The California Trail

The California Trail opened in 1841. It wasn't popular at first. The trail was dangerous. The route began along the Oregon Trail. But, near Idaho, the two trails split. If travelers wanted to go north, they took the Oregon Trail. Going south took them along the California Trail. After the split, people had to travel through deserts in Utah and Nevada. Then, they had to cross the Sierra Nevada Mountains. It has some of the tallest mountains in the country! It took months to cross the Sierras. Getting caught in the snow had deadly consequences. Even with the dangers of the trail, people were still willing to try.

In 1848, James Marshall discovered gold in California. News spread across the country. Many people thought they could get rich quick. By the next year, 80,000 people had moved to California. They were called 49ers. Many of them had used the California and Oregon trails. Over the next 5 years, more than 250,000 people made the dangerous journey. Some traveled all the way from Europe! Slowly, the gold ran out and the California Gold Rush came to an end. Yet many people stayed.

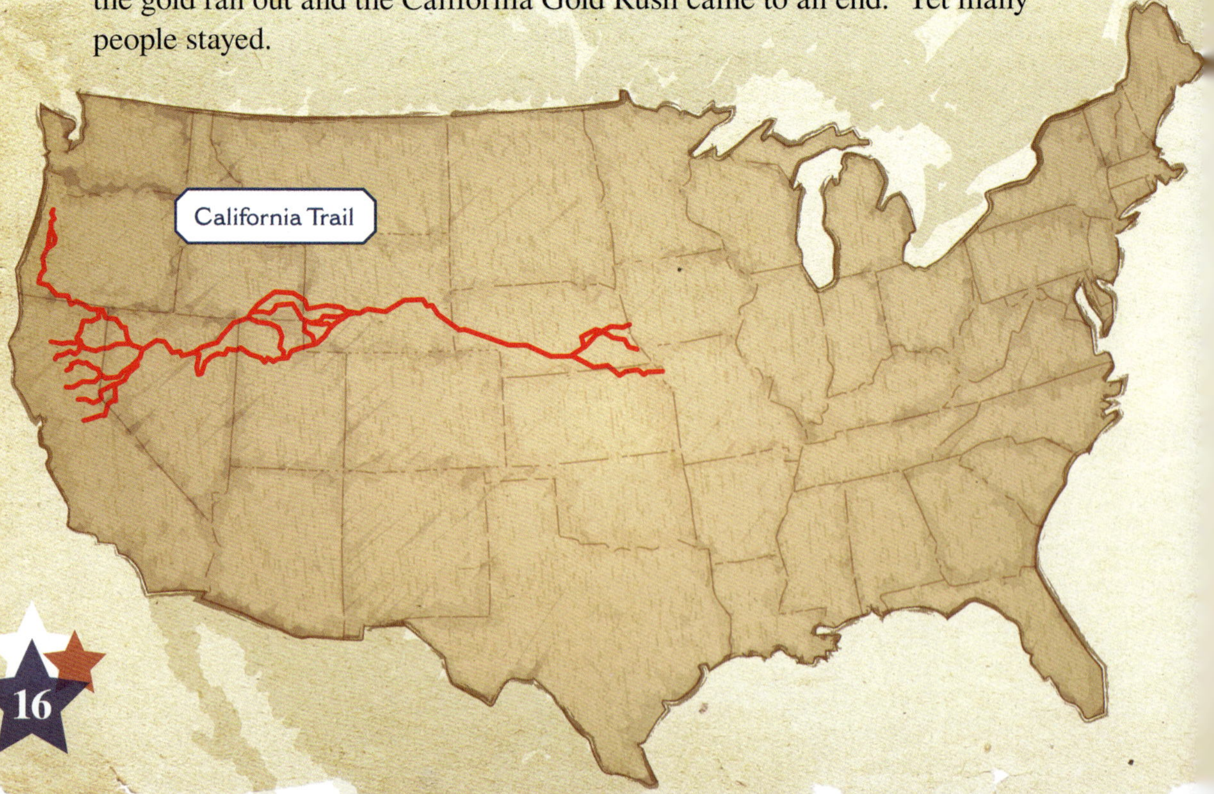

Sierra Nevada mountain range

THE CALIFORNIA HERALD.

NEW YORK, TUESDAY, DECEMBER 26, 1848.

This 1848 newspaper describes the discovery of gold in California.

49ERS

Many **pioneers** headed to California when news spread that gold had been discovered. By the time most of them had arrived, it was 1849. Americans began referring to these gold-seeking pioneers as 49ers and the name stuck.

A 49er pans for gold in California.

Mormon pioneers journey to Salt Lake City.

Joseph Smith

Brigham Young

The Mormon Trail

When Joseph Smith founded the **Mormon** religion in 1830, it grew quickly. But, many people did not like the new religion. They didn't like that Mormons practiced **polygamy**. And the quick spread of the new religion scared many people. They burned Mormon homes and farms. In 1846, Smith was killed by an angry mob. After that, many Mormons decided it was time to move. They wanted to go west. The route they took is known as the Mormon Trail.

Brigham Young became the leader of the Mormon religion after Smith. He led 3,000 people west in February of 1846. They hoped to make it to Utah before the next winter came. But it was still very cold. There was too much ice and snow for them to travel safely. So, they decided to stop at the Missouri River for a few months. On July 24, 1847, the first group of Mormons arrived in Salt Lake City, Utah. They had left their homes more than a year before. Over the next 20 years, nearly 70,000 Mormons crossed the Mormon Trail.

As more settlers headed west, the United States continued to expand. The young country was growing in size and strength. But, this fast growth caused problems with the people already living there.

Unsettling the West

Not everyone was pleased that people were moving west. American Indians had been living on the land for thousands of years. As settlers moved, they wanted more and more land. They thought it was their destiny. So, they kicked American Indians out. As the country grew, tribes lost millions of acres.

In 1830, President Andrew Jackson signed the Indian Removal Act. It made Eastern tribes move west of the Mississippi River. Now, they had to live on land called **reservations**. Once they were there, they were not allowed to leave. Over the next 20 years, nearly 100,000 American Indians were forced to move west. And more settlers kept coming. The United States took more and more tribal land. They forced tribes to stay in smaller and smaller areas. Many tribes decided to fight back.

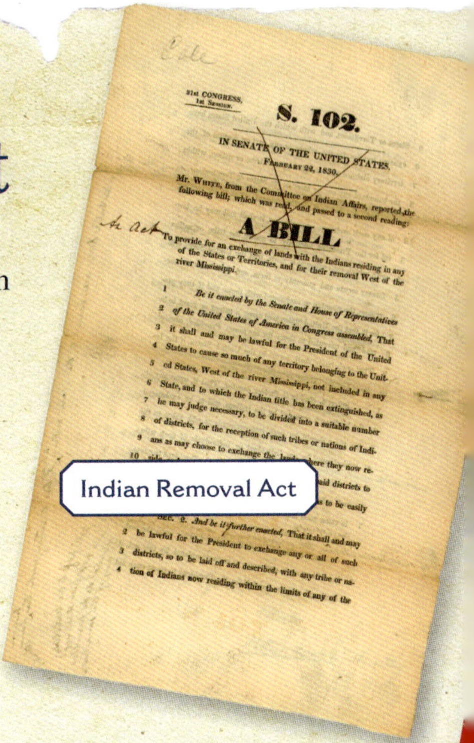

21st CONGRESS, 1st Session.

S. 102.

IN SENATE OF THE UNITED STATES.

February 22, 1830.

Mr. White, from the Committee on Indian Affairs, reported the following bill; which was read, and passed to a second reading:

A BILL

To provide for an exchange of lands with the Indians residing in any of the States or Territories, and for their removal West of the river Mississippi.

Be it enacted by the Senate and House of Representatives of the United States of America in Congress assembled, That it shall and may be lawful for the President of the United States to cause so much of any territory belonging to the United States, West of the river Mississippi, not included in any State, and to which the Indian title has been extinguished, as he may judge necessary, to be divided into a suitable number of districts, for the reception of such tribes or nations of Indians as may choose to exchange the lands where they now re- … said districts to … to be easily

Sec. 2. *And be it further enacted,* That it shall and may be lawful for the President to exchange any or all of such districts, so to be laid off and described, with any tribe or nation of Indians now residing within the limits of any of the

Indian Removal Act

INDIAN LAND FOR SALE

GET A HOME OF YOUR OWN

EASY PAYMENTS

PERFECT TITLE

POSSESSION WITHIN THIRTY DAYS

FINE LANDS IN THE WEST

IRRIGATED IRRIGABLE GRAZING AGRICULTURAL DRY FARMING

In 1910 the Department of the Interior Sold Under Sealed Bids Allotted Indian Land as Follows:

Location.	Acres.	Average Price per Acre.	Location.	Acres.	Average Price per Acre.
Colorado	5,211.21	$7.27	Oklahoma	34,664.00	$19.14
Idaho	17,013.00	24.85	Oregon	1,020.00	15.43
Kansas	1,684.50	33.45	South Dakota	120,445.00	16.53
Montana	11,034.00	9.86	Washington	4,879.00	41.37
Nebraska	5,641.00	36.65	Wisconsin	1,069.00	17.00
North Dakota	22,610.70	9.93	Wyoming	865.00	20.64

FOR THE YEAR 1911 IT IS ESTIMATED THAT 350,000 ACRES WILL BE OFFERED FOR SALE

For information as to the character of the land write for booklet, "INDIAN LANDS FOR SALE," to the Superintendent U. S. Indian School at any one of the following places:

WALTER L. FISHER, Secretary of the Interior

ROBERT G. VALENTINE, Commissioner of Indian Affairs

GRAND RUSH FOR THE INDIAN TERRITORY!

NOW IS THE CHANCE TO PROCURE A HOME

In this Beautiful Country!

Over 15,000,000 Acres of Land NOW OPEN FOR SETTLEMENT!

Being part of the Land bought by the Government in 1866 from the Indians for the Freedmen.

THE FINEST TIMBER! THE RICHEST LAND! THE FINEST WATERED! WEST OF THE MISSISSIPPI RIVER.

The Grand Expedition will Leave Independence May 7, 1879

ABOUT THE LANDS.

ADDRESS WM. C. BRANHAM, Independence, Kansas.

These documents advertise land that used to belong to American Indians.

American Indians walk the Trail of Tears.

TRAIL OF TEARS

The Cherokee tribe was forced to walk 800 mi. (1,300 km) to their new reservations. Almost one-third of the original 15,000 died from hunger or disease along the way. This walk became known as the Trail of Tears.

Many battles were fought between the U.S. government and the tribes. Some were fought when people refused to leave their homes. That was the case with the three Seminole Wars. The Seminole tribe refused to leave Florida and live on reservations. When soldiers arrived, the people fought back. But they were outnumbered. By 1858, almost all Seminoles had left Florida.

Other wars were fought when settlers tried to take over American Indian land. Red Cloud was a Lakota war chief. When gold was discovered in Montana in 1863, the government tried to set up a trail through his tribe's land. So, the tribe fought back. After two years, the government withdrew. They agreed that the Lakota owned the land. But peace did not last long.

In 1874, gold was again found on Lakota land. The government tried to force the Lakota to move. When the tribe refused, General Custer came up with a plan. On June 25, 1876, he attacked the tribe in what became known as the Battle of the Little Bighorn. But, Custer's soldiers were outnumbered and unprepared. He and all his men were killed. After that, U.S. troops swarmed the region and sent the tribe to a reservation.

A FAMILY AFFAIR

George Armstrong Custer and four members of his family were killed at the Battle of the Little Bighorn. Today, the Battle of the Little Bighorn is also called Custer's Last Stand.

U.S. soldiers capture Seminole chiefs.

Chief Red Cloud

Battle of the Little Bighorn

Many tribes were angry with the U.S. government. They had been forced off their lands and made to head west. The government often broke treaties with tribes to take more land. Still, nomadic Plains tribes were able to avoid the government's reach more easily. They moved from place to place in search of buffalo. Tribes relied on buffalo for food. So, the government devised a plan. They encouraged settlers to hunt buffalo for sport. If they killed enough of them, the tribes would be forced to move to reservations.

Tribes only killed what they needed. But, settlers killed many more. Sometimes, they took buffalo hides and sold them. Other times, they just left the dead buffalo along the trails. In 1800, there were over 80 million buffalo living in the United States. By 1900, there were only 500 left. Because of this tactic, buffalo almost went extinct. Many tribes suffered. They joined other tribes on reservations. Settlers rushed to claim the new land in the name of destiny.

Americans shoot buffalo from a train.

American Indian camp in 1848

A Growing Nation

The 1800s were a time of growth for the United States. As more people moved west, travel changed. Trails were cleared and new routes were discovered. In 1869, the first railroad to stretch from the East to the West was completed. This made travel much faster and safer. The trails were used less and less. **Settlements** sprang up along the railroads. People settled into their new homes in the West. The possibilities seemed endless.

The transcontinental railroad passes through a small town in the 1800s.

But, the settling of the West also caused many problems. The United States was at odds with Great Britain yet again. And, a war with Mexico left Mexicans angry at the United States. These feelings would take many years to fade. American Indians lost their homes when they were forced to move. And the buffalo population was almost completely wiped out.

The new country explored its borders in the 1800s. Twenty-eight new states were added. Suddenly, the United States was one of the largest countries in the world. And it was still growing.

This map shows the growth of the United States from 1783 to 1853.

Advertise It!

Getting what you needed to survive on the frontier wasn't always easy. There were few stores in the West. Storeowners had to carry many products for their customers. Frontier stores often sold everything from food to medicine to wagon parts.

Imagine you are a storeowner on the frontier. What will you stock? What might pioneers need that they can't get on their own? Create an advertisement for your store. Include popular items and drawings of what your store carries. Then, give your store a catchy name. Share your poster with friends and family members.

NEW
Cheap Store!!

BOOT, SHOE & SLIPPER
Manufactory.

THE subscriber would inform the citizens of ALTON, and vicinity, that he has taken the STORE under the "*Telegraph*" Office, Second Street, where he has on hand, a good assortment of

GROCERIES,
Boots & Shoes,

Of all kinds and qualities; and will be receiving FRESH GOODS from time to time; and manufacturing BOOTS, SHOES, and SLIPPERS, daily: so that he will be able to keep a *supply constantly on hand*, to accommodate all those who may favor him with their patronage. ☞*Prices Low, in accordance with the times.*☜

N. B.---Those who wish to *Economize* these *hard times*, will please to call at the sign of the ☞"*Golden Slipper,*"☜ where I shall sell VERY LOW for *Cash* or *Country Produce;* and all Goods are *Warranted*, and *rips mended gratis.*

SAM'L LESURE.

Alton, Sept. 13, 1841.

Printed at the "Telegraph" office---Alton.

NEW LIST OF PRICES
HOOP SKIRTS, THREADS, CORSETS,
TRIMMINGS, HOSIERY, BUTTONS,
Fancy Goods and Small Wares,
CHEAP STORE
98 DUDLEY STREET, 98
BOSTON HIGHLANDS.
PRICES LOWER THAN EVER
ONLY 5 CENTS A SPOOL
HOOP SKIRTS!
MISSES HOOP SKIRTS
CORSETS!
HOSIERY.
BUTTONS! BUTTONS!
Cluny, Saxony, and Crochet Edgings,
DON'T MISTAKE THE PLACE.
98 DUDLEY STREET, 98
BOSTON HIGHLANDS,

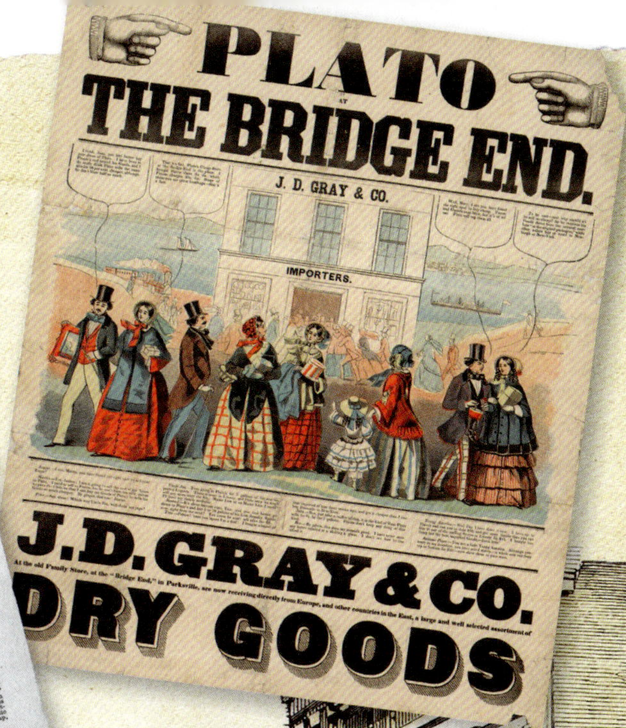
PLATO
AT
THE BRIDGE END.
J. D. GRAY & CO.
IMPORTERS.
J.D.GRAY&CO.
DRY GOODS

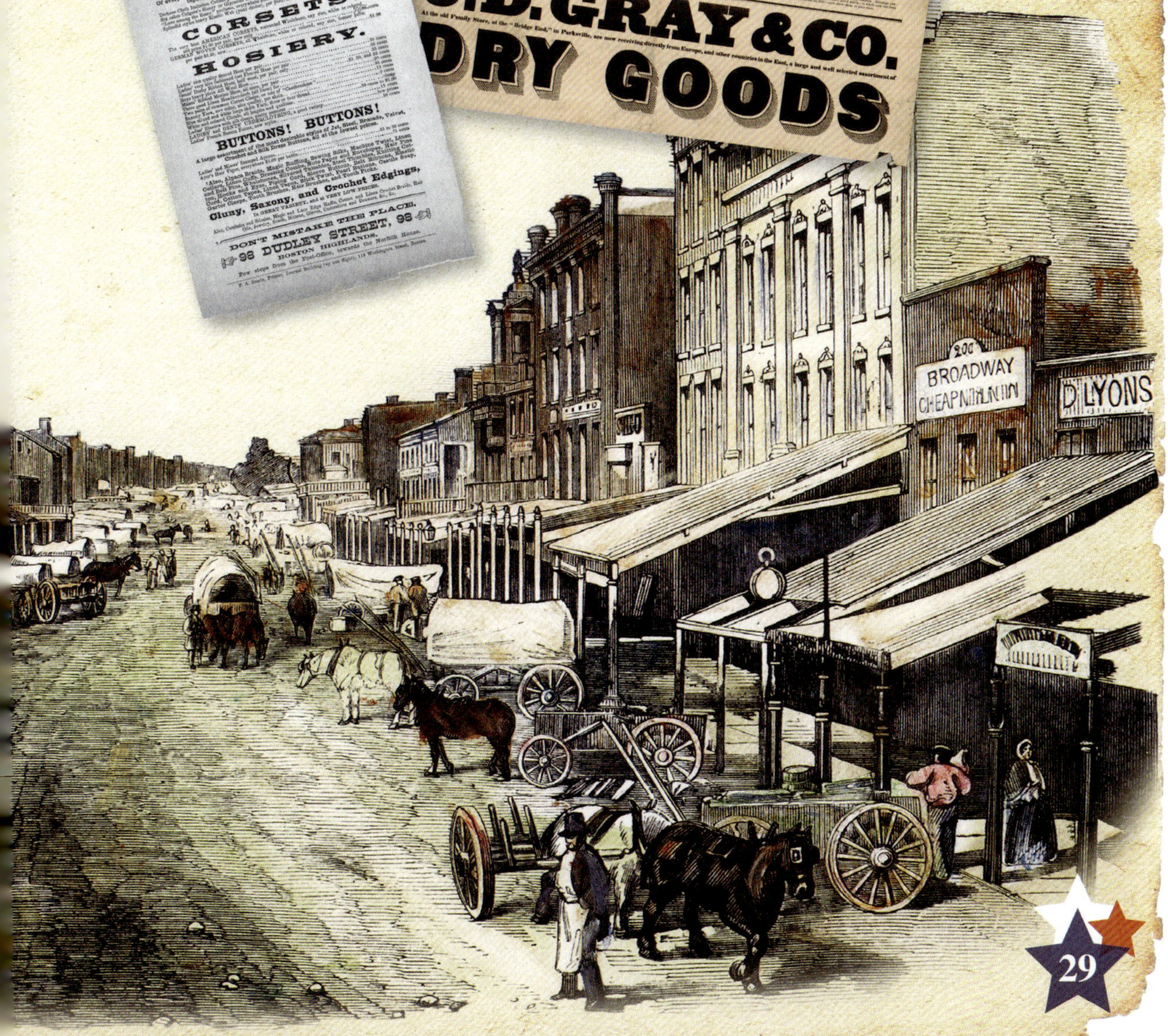
200
BROADWAY
D LYONS

Glossary

annexed—added a territory or place to a country

emigrants—people who leave a country or region to live elsewhere

fertile—capable of supporting the growth of many plants

frontier—an area where few people live

homestead—land people acquired from the government by farming and living on it

Manifest Destiny—the idea that the United States had a right to extend its borders to the Pacific Ocean

Mormon—a member of a Christian church founded by Joseph Smith

oppressed—treated a person or group of people in a cruel or unfair way

pioneers—people who are the first to explore and settle a new place

polygamy—the act of being married to more than one person at the same time

pull factors—the advantages of a place that make people want to move there

push factors—the disadvantages of a place that make people want to move away

reservations—areas of land in the United States for American Indians to live

settlements—places where people have come to live and where few people lived before

trade route—a course followed by traders and merchants

treaty—a formal agreement made between two or more countries or groups

tribes—groups of people who have the same language, customs, and beliefs

Index

49ers, 16–17

American Indians, 4, 7, 20–22, 25, 27

California Gold Rush, 16

California Trail, 16

Custer, George Armstrong, 22

Great Britain, 4, 12, 27

Jackson, Andrew, 20

Lincoln, Abraham, 8

Little Bighorn, Battle of the, 22–23

Manifest Destiny, 6–7

Mexicans, 4, 14–15, 27

Mormon Trail, 19

O'Sullivan, John, 6–7

Oregon Trail, 12–14, 16

railroad, 26

Red Cloud, 22–23

Santa Fe Trail, 14

Seminole Wars, 22

Smith, Joseph, 18–19

Trail of Tears, 21

Young, Brigham, 18–19

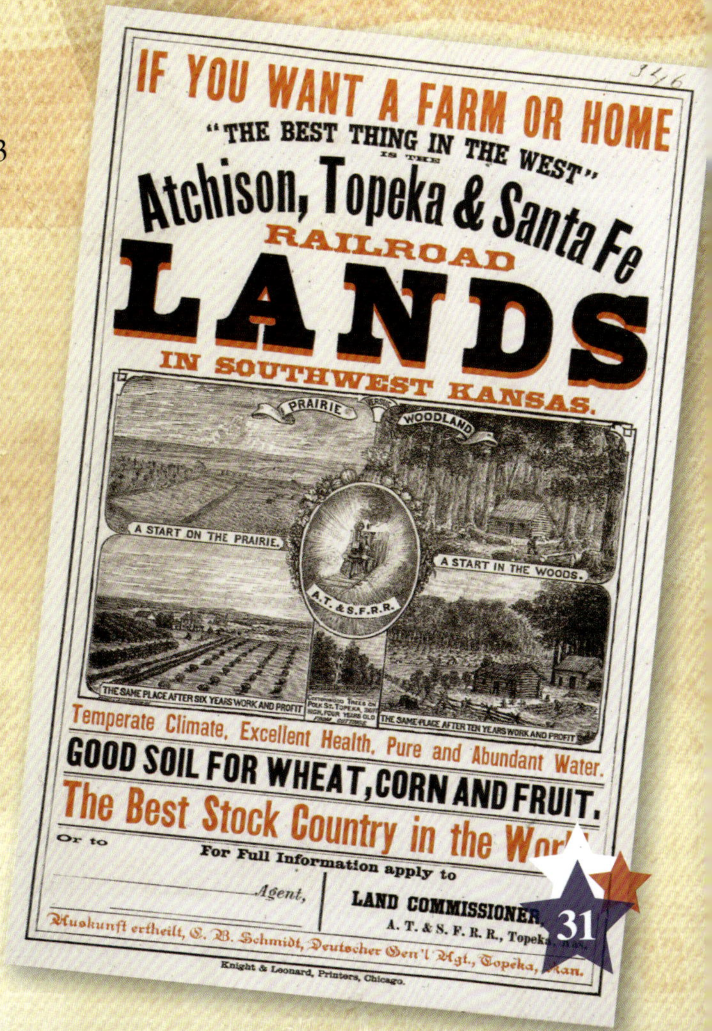

Your Turn!

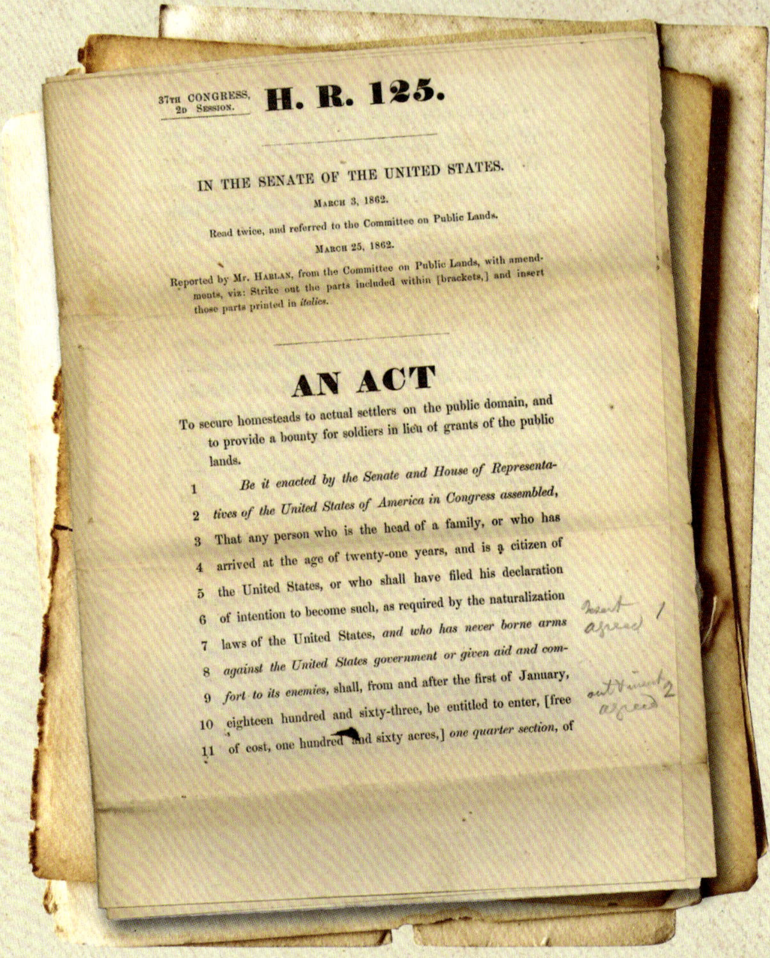

37TH CONGRESS, 2D SESSION. **H. R. 125.**

IN THE SENATE OF THE UNITED STATES.

MARCH 3, 1862.

Read twice, and referred to the Committee on Public Lands.

MARCH 25, 1862.

Reported by Mr. HARLAN, from the Committee on Public Lands, with amendments, viz: Strike out the parts included within [brackets,] and insert those parts printed in *italics*.

AN ACT

To secure homesteads to actual settlers on the public domain, and to provide a bounty for soldiers in lieu of grants of the public lands.

Be it enacted by the Senate and House of Representatives of the United States of America in Congress assembled, That any person who is the head of a family, or who has arrived at the age of twenty-one years, and is a citizen of the United States, or who shall have filed his declaration of intention to become such, as required by the naturalization laws of the United States, *and who has never borne arms against the United States government or given aid and comfort to its enemies,* shall, from and after the first of January, eighteen hundred and sixty-three, be entitled to enter, [free of cost, one hundred and sixty acres,] *one quarter section,* of

Stay or Go?

The Homestead Act was a major pull factor in the 1800s. It encouraged many people to settle the frontier. Moving west was not easy, though. And once settlers arrived, they had to start new lives. Write a list of pros and cons that settlers might have considered when making the decision to move west.